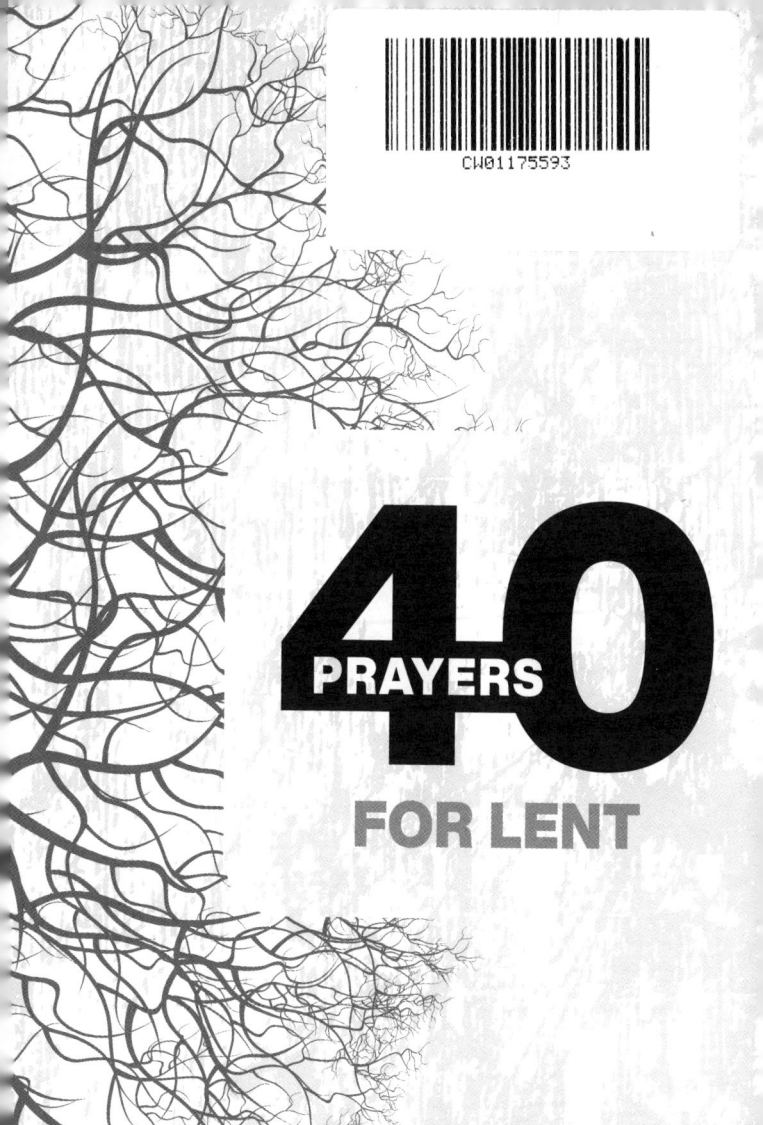

40 PRAYERS
FOR LENT

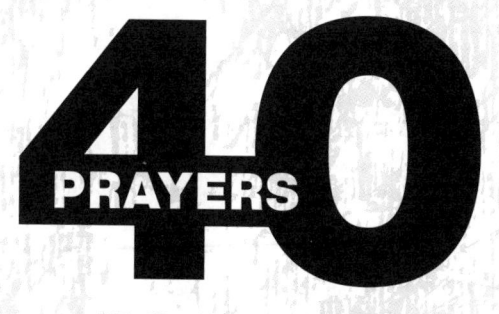

40 PRAYERS
FOR LENT

Prayers for your
Church or small group

DAVID CLOWES

DAVID C COOK
transforming lives together

40 PRAYERS FOR LENT
Published by David C Cook
4050 Lee Vance Drive
Colorado Springs, CO 80918 U.S.A.

Integrity Music Limited, a Division of David C Cook
Brighton, East Sussex BN1 2RE, England

The graphic circle C logo is a registered trademark of David C Cook.

All rights reserved. Except for brief excerpts for review purposes, no part of this book may be reproduced or used in any form without written permission from the publisher.

The website addresses recommended throughout this book are offered as a resource to you. These websites are not intended in any way to be or imply an endorsement on the part of David C Cook, nor do we vouch for their content.

ISBN 978-0-8307-8234-5
eISBN 978-0-8307-8242-0

© 2021 David Clowes

The Team: Ian Matthews, Jack Campbell,
Jo Stockdale, Susan Murdock
Cover Design: Pete Barnsley

Printed in the United Kingdom
First Edition 2021

1 2 3 4 5 6 7 8 9 10

120120

CONTENTS

Introduction 7

Prayers of Approach 9

Prayers of Praise 12

Prayers of Thanksgiving 19

Prayers of Confession 28

Prayers for All Ages 32

Prayers of Intercession 38

Prayers of Commitment 52

Prayers of Dismissal 54

About the Author 56

INTRODUCTION

Having published *500 Prayers for All Occasions* and *500 More Prayers for All Occasions* I was asked to develop a new series of books of prayer for use in small groups or in the home.

There are at least forty prayers in each of these books based around a single theme. Most of the content comes from my first two books of prayer for public worship, but has been revised and re-worked to make it appropriate for use in churches, small groups, the family situation, or for personal quiet time devotions.

My church background was firmly in the camp of extemporary prayer. I started to write my prayers down due to nervousness and on the advice of my preaching mentor who insisted on careful preparation not only of the hymns, readings, and sermon, but also of the prayers. I have long since realised the value of having a resource to be used as a flexible launch pad for my own prayer life which I could use and adapt as I wished.

I hope that is how you will approach these simple aids to prayer. They have been deliberately written in an uncomplicated style and with language that seeks to illuminate the joy of prayer. I have also tried to ensure that they are written in the language we use in our daily conversations. The aim of this is designed to make them easier to 'pray' and not simply to 'read'.

David Clowes
Stockport, April 2020

PRAYERS OF APPROACH

KNOWING YOU LOVE US

Father, we come as your children knowing you love us.
We come with no hope of proving our worth.
We come as those who through grace
you have already accepted to worship you,
    our Saviour and Lord.
We come knowing our strengths and our weaknesses
to the one who holds all things by
    the power of his word.
We come to sing glory for the life, love, and joy
of knowing Jesus, the Saviour of all. **Amen.**

OUR STRENGTH

Lord, we come to you because you are strength
    for us when our strength fails;
you are hope for us when our hope is gone;
you are love for us when we are cold and empty;
you are forgiveness for us when we go wrong;
you are peace for us when we are afraid;
you are beginning again when it feels like the end.
We come to worship you because
    you are worthy. **Amen.**

OUT OF THE DARKNESS

Lord, we come out of our darkness and into your light.
We come out of our emptiness to enter your fullness.
We come out of our hopelessness to find your joy.
We come out of our confusion to seek your peace.
We come far from home because we
    know we have been found.
We come at your invitation to praise you as Lord. **Amen.**

TRANSFIGURATION

Father,
coming into your presence is like
    stepping out of deep darkness
into the blinding sun.
You overwhelm us by your glory, your
    power, and your majesty.
We cannot hope to comprehend the
    wonder of your glory.
But we have come to be warmed by your grace,
transformed by your mercy, set free by your love,
and to worship you in the power of the Spirit. **Amen.**

THE VICTORY OF THE CROSS

Father, we come to you in the name of Jesus.
We come trusting that you will accept
    us and our worship.
We come in the assurance of the love
he demonstrated in his death on the cross.
Keep convincing us of your love,
    softening our hard hearts,
and bringing us to the foot of his cross
that we might be prepared to carry the
    cross for his glory. **Amen.**

THE WAY OF THE CROSS

Father, we come to you not because we
    are good enough to come
or because we have anything of our own to give you.
We come to confess that everything
everywhere belongs to you, including ourselves.
We come, not simply because it is our duty to come,
but because we long to offer you our worship.
We come with joy and thankfulness
because Jesus has opened the way into your presence.
We come to crown him as King of our lives
and to praise him as Lord of all. **Amen.**

PRAYERS OF PRAISE

YOU SHARED EVERYTHING

Almighty God, our heavenly Father,
we praise you that in Christ you have
    entered into our world.
In him you have shared all the pressure,
    pain, and temptation
that being truly human brings.

We praise you that we can have assurance
that he fully understands all that it
    means to live in our world.
He has lived our life, shared our emptiness,
    and experienced our limitations.
We praise you that he has walked where
    we walk but he did not stumble;
that he has stood where we stand but did not fall;
that he entered our wilderness but did not give way;
and that he faced our temptations but did not give in.

We praise you that in the wilderness,
in Gethsemane, and on the cross,
Christ has opened the way to victory and hope.
We praise you that in his life, death, and resurrection

you are offering us a whole new way of
>   life, a deeper, larger hope,
and an assurance of your presence for ever. **Amen.**

WONDERFUL GOD

Wonderful God!
We praise you for bringing light into our darkness
and joy into our sorrow;
for filling our lives when we feel empty
and for guiding us when we are lost.
We praise you for restoring us when we are broken
and for holding us when we are hurting;
for giving us life and for creating a world
>   of such beauty and variety.
We praise you for every opportunity
to experience something of the riches around us
and for giving us eyes to see the wonders you have made,
ears to hear the music of life, and
>   voices to give you the glory.

Wonderful God!
We praise you for the utter assurance
>   of your total dependability.
You never change; you are always
>   reaching out in love for those
whose lives are a poor imitation of all
>   that you meant them to be.
We praise you, great God, that you are;
your love is for those who are lost, afraid, and defeated
by all that life throws against them.
We praise you for Christ who set his face like flint
in his determination to face the conflict of life for us.
We praise you that through his sacrificial
>   death and his glorious resurrection

he has shown us the full measure of your love
> that will never be defeated. **Amen.**

IN THE DARKNESS

Almighty God, our heavenly Father, we
> praise you that you are with us
not simply when life is easy and carefree
but in the darkness, the emptiness,
and those times when we feel lost and uncertain.
We praise you that though you have never
> promised that life would be easy,
without pain or problems, you have assured
> us that you will be with us.
We praise you that no matter who we are,
> where we go, or what we face,
your almighty presence never leaves us.
We praise you for your gentle understanding
> of our doubts and our fears,
and most of all for Jesus Christ and
> for the way that, in him,
you shared in our suffering.
We praise you that you are not a God who is content
to sit on the sidelines of life.
In Christ you entered into our world of pain and loss.
We praise you that he is the only one who can say
that he does know how we feel
and that he fully understands what life is costing us.
We remember how he began life in
> the poverty of a stable.
Through his life he was dependent on others
for friendship and food, for anointing and the donkey,
for a cross and a tomb.
Lord, help us to praise him even when
> we are alone or afraid,

rejected or overwhelmed by demands made upon us,
lost or frustrated, confused or just hurting.
Help us to praise him for he enters
    even our pain. **Amen.**

INCREDIBLE GOD

Incredible God!
We praise you for the way
you can take the ordinary things and make them new;
that you are able to take ordinary lives,
lived by ordinary people, and fill them with meaning.
We praise you for your promise of joy
and your offer of peace that can utterly transform
how we live and respond.
We praise you for Jesus who walked a
    hard path through his life;
for the way he shared in the hopes
and the fears of those around him;
for the way he makes us aware of the
    demands of your love;
and for the way that his presence still
    breaks hardened hearts.
We praise you for the way Christ touches
    and changes the whole of life.
He opens our eyes to the wonder of your creation
and our ears to the songs of your love.
He opens our lips to praise you
for his coming, living, dying, and his rising.
He opens our hearts to receive him
and to be filled with his life-transforming Spirit.

Incredible God!
There is no God like you, no God besides you.
You are Lord of the whole of creation.

The universe is not large enough to contain
> the praise we want to offer you.
We praise you for Christ the door
and the key to new life, new beginning,
> and wholeness for ever.
In his name and for his glory. **Amen.**

GLIMPSE OF YOUR HOPE

Father, we praise you for Jesus Christ.
We praise you for the life he lived
> and the teaching he gave;
for the way he made your love real and
> your truth understandable;
for his death in our place on the cross
> made by our sinfulness.
We praise you that through his acceptance
> of others' cruel words and actions
he has made it possible for us to see your mercy.
We praise you that through his refusal
> to compromise with evil
we are brought face to face with your holiness.
We praise you that through his experience
> of our emptiness and desolation
we are given a glimpse of your hope.
We praise you that through his dying
we are offered the chance of forgiveness and peace.
We praise you that through his mighty resurrection
we are given the promise of heaven and your eternal love.
Father, our Father, we have so much to praise you for
and we will do so for ever.
For we praise you in Jesus;
for in him all our praises have their beginning
and by your Spirit they will know no ending. **Amen.**

IT'S PALM SUNDAY

Father, we praise you for your glory which we have seen
in the life, death, and resurrection of
> Jesus Christ, our Lord.
We join in the praises of those who greeted
> him as he rode into Jerusalem
and for his coming on the back of a donkey,
the sign that he comes as the Prince of Peace.
We praise you that in his coming
you have demonstrated not only your commitment to us
but your total rejection of all that is evil,
and for the utter determination of your
> love to touch our hearts,
to change our lives, and to gently, but
> firmly, call us to follow your Son.

We praise you that even when the world
> and our neighbours have,
like the crowds of Palm Sunday, stopped
> praising him, he is still Lord;
that even when those around us,
like the mob who cried crucify, turn their backs on you
and reject your Son and your purpose
> of grace for a lost world,
still you cannot be defeated.

We praise you that whether,
like the crowds who waved their palm branches,
we are passing through times of peace and rejoicing
or whether it feels as if we are standing
> at the foot of a cross,
and life seems dark, and it feels as if
> we have reached the end.

Whatever we are facing, you give us the assurance
that your grace is sufficient.

We praise you for the victory of your love
that triumphed over sin and death.
We praise you that now and always he is our living Lord.
We come to praise you now in and for him
as we will praise you for all eternity. **Amen.**

PRAYERS OF THANKSGIVING

STANDING FIRM

Father, we thank you for your Son, Jesus Christ,
who faced all the temptations that come to us all.
We thank you more for the assurance
   that in him temptation
can be defeated and that we can live victorious
   lives for him and through him.
We thank you for those who have heard the call of Christ
and by faith have stood firm in him.
We thank you for those who have remained faithful
to what they knew to be true
even at the cost of the support of family and friends.
We praise you for those who have
   faced all kinds of pressure
and persecution for their faith in Christ,
who refused to deny him as their Saviour and Lord.
We praise you for those who have stood against
injustice and oppression,
who have faced deep disappointment and frustration
but have preferred to walk with Christ
   rather than the crowd.
We thank you for the assurance that in the cross of Christ
and in his resurrection from the dead

we can overcome all our trials and temptations
through him who has won the victory. **Amen.**

THE JOY OF LIFE

Almighty God, our heavenly Father, we
 have come to worship you,
to praise you, and to honour your name,
and to thank you for the wonder and the joy of life;
for every opportunity to serve you and to give you glory.
Thank you that every time we think we
 understand who you are,
you break the limits of our minds with your sovereignty;
every time we think we understand your ways,
you astound us again with your majesty;
every time we think you are above and beyond us,
you invade our hearts and minds;
every time we think we can reduce you
 to a size we can control,
you slip through our grasp
and leave us overwhelmed with your holiness and love.
Lord, by your power the world has its being,
through your grace our lives are made new.
Thank you for the mystery of your love
at the heart of all creation that gives us hope,
heals our lives, and gives us strength.
Lord, we thank you for every person
who battles against all that spoils your world,
damages your creation, and limits human freedom.
We thank you for those who fight to conquer
all that is wrong, all that is evil,
and all that is against your will for your creation.
We thank you that in the midst of all our conflicts,
through Christ's life on earth and his ministry in the world,
you have demonstrated your love for us all. **Amen.**

THE PATH OF FAITH

You are truly an amazing God!
We thank you for every person who has
 walked the path of faith.
For those whose trust in you, no matter the cost,
and who have been an encouragement to others.
We thank you for those whose faith has enabled them
to be lifted above their pain and suffering
and whose lives have been filled with gentleness,
 hope, grace, peace, and joy.
We thank you for all those whose quality of life,
even through their suffering, has reminded us
that life is more than health and strength.
We thank you that you do not send our hurt or our pain
and that you never intended us to suffer
 or to experience great loss.
We thank you more that you take every
 experience of our lives,
every twist and turn that we face, and
by your grace you offer to transform it into
 an opportunity to begin again.
We thank you for Jesus, the only true source of your grace.
We thank you for the hard lesson that
 new life comes through death,
that hope is your offer for all in despair,
and love is your promise for ever. **Amen.**

WITHOUT LIMIT

Father, we thank you that there is no limit to your power
to make all things new;
for mercy that is always seeking the lost
and bringing them home.
We thank you for your pity that walks with us
and holds us and loves us and accepts us still;

for your grace that never
lets us off, never lets us down, and never lets us go.
We thank you for Christ in whom your life-changing,
world-renewing love is made known;
for all those who,
down the centuries and across the world,
have lived bravely for your truth;
for those whose commitment
has opened other people's eyes to your presence;
for those whose witness, faithfulness, and love
make yesterday bearable, tomorrow hopeful,
    and today liveable.
We thank you for the transfiguration of Jesus;
for the way the eyes of his disciples were opened
to begin to understand something
    more of who he really was.
We thank you for those moments
    when you have broken into
our thoughts, our hearts, and our lives
and revealed something more of your lordship,
your power, your love, and your glory.
We thank you for the blazing light of the Holy Spirit
who transforms our frustration,
    our darkness, and our emptiness
with the power of his presence and makes our lives whole.
Thank you, Lord, for every person who has
spoken your name, demonstrated your love,
and made us open to your guidance and glory.
In the name of Jesus, who changes everything. **Amen.**

OUR LIFE TOGETHER IN CHRIST

Sovereign Lord, we thank you for our
    life together in Christ.
It is in him and through him that we have been made one.

We thank you that though we are all very different people,
that though we come from different places
and have different hopes and fears,
different thoughts and expectations, yet we are one in Christ
because you have made us so.
We thank you for all you have given us
    as your children of grace.
Thank you for the hope, the joy, the peace, and the love
with which you have flooded our lives.
We thank you for the new sense of
    meaning, purpose, and direction
with which you have touched our lives.
We thank you for the new awareness of your presence
in every moment of our lives, in the whole of creation,
and in our fellowship together.
We thank you for the joy we have received
    from family and friends
and through the wonder of your creation.
We thank you for those whose love and kindness
have changed our lives, our attitudes, and our hearts.
We thank you for the knowledge that Christ is our Saviour
and that Jesus is Lord.
We thank you for your hope for the future,
your cleansing for the past,
and your power and presence for today.
We thank you and ask that by your Holy Spirit
we may live, speak, and act as your thankful
    people every day of our lives.
In the name of Christ who makes us one. **Amen.**

NEVER DEFEATED

Father, we thank you for your love
which will never be lost and never be defeated
and for your grace and mercy that will never end,

because like you they have no beginning.
We thank you that though Jesus received
    the praise of the crowds
he was not swayed by it
because of his total knowledge of you
and what we are and what we are capable of.
We thank you that though our
    commitment is unreliable,
you still call us to follow Christ and know him as Saviour.
We thank you that though you are not fooled
by our empty promises of obedience and trust,
you continue to call us to carry a cross
    and accept him as Lord.
We thank you for all whose lives are an
    example of faithful perseverance
in their commitment to Christ
and for those whose worship, service, and trust
have far outlasted all the passing thrills
    that come with Palm Sunday.
We thank you for those whose lives of loving
    obedience told us most clearly
that they knew you as Saviour
and for those whose faithful witness to Jesus
brought us to know him as our living Lord.
We thank you that though your cross looked
    like the end of the celebration,
through his resurrection and the coming of the Spirit
you have turned the end into a new beginning.
We thank you that in him, one day,
you will gather up all our feeble attempts
at praising and serving and trusting and loving
and call us to join in a song that has no ending. **Amen.**

MAUNDY THURSDAY

Father, our Father, we thank you for your
    Son, Jesus Christ our Lord;
for his faithfulness to the task that you gave him
and for his obedience to your will for his life;
for his grace and kindness to those around him
and for his love for those who betrayed him,
    rejected him, and crucified him.

We thank you that he is for us
a picture of your endless loving-kindness;
that your love is not something simply to know about
but to be experienced in our own lives;
that your grace and mercy are not just words in the Bible
but can be a reality in our own hearts.

We thank you for the way Jesus washed the disciples' feet
and for his example of care, compassion, and servanthood;
for his challenge to us to love one another
    just as he has loved us;
for his acceptance even of Judas
and that not even his act of betrayal could
    prevent Jesus from loving him.

We thank you that he took the bread and the wine
and transformed them into symbols of
    his death for us on the cross;
that through the Holy Spirit we can
    know his presence and power
and serve in his name and for his glory each day.
Father, we bring our prayer of thanks in the
    name of the Servant King. **Amen.**

GOOD FRIDAY

Father, we thank you for who and what you are
and for what you have done for us and in us;
that though you are our mighty
   creator and sovereign Lord
you are also the God whose nature is love.
We thank you for your holiness
and for your utter purity which is
   clothed with love and mercy.
You are the righteous one.
You are always in the right and you
   always do what is right.
There is absolutely nothing that is unrighteous in you.
We thank you that you are not only a God of justice
but also a God of deep compassion
whose understanding knows no bounds.
Sovereign Lord, you reign supreme in eternity
and yet you are never far from us.
You are for ever above and beyond us
and yet in Christ you came and lived
   our life and died our death.
Lord, we thank you for all you have done for us
in and through your Son, Jesus Christ, our Lord. **Amen.**

THE ACHIEVEMENT OF THE CROSS

On this Good Friday, we thank you for his
   death on the cross of Calvary
and that through him we can know our sins are forgiven
and be assured that we are accepted.
Father, again and again you astound us with your love
that overwhelms our sin and our self-centredness.
In Jesus you have wiped the slate clean,
you have given us a new page in the book of our lives
and have given us the opportunity to begin again.

We thank you that when Jesus said, 'It is finished!'
he assured us that there is nothing we
    can do, nothing we can add
to what he has already done to open
    the way to life that is real,
life that is lived in the knowledge of your presence.
Father, our Father, we thank you and we praise you
as we stand at the foot of the cross
and confess that he is the Lord and there is no other.
In the name of the Saviour of the world. **Amen.**

PRAYERS OF CONFESSION

VALUES OF THE KINGDOM

Lord, we confess that we pay lip service
    to the values of your kingdom.
We love those who love us, but we find it
    impossible even to like our enemies.
We are honest and faithful if the cost is not too high.
We confess that too easily we accept
    the standards of the world
and not those of Christ.
We have settled for justice instead of caring concern
and for fair play when you called us to love.
We have exchanged what is right for what seems to work
and what is true for what does not hurt.
We allow the world to set the example
    instead of our Lord.
Forgive us, Lord, that our striving
    against temptation is so weak
and our struggle for what is right is so short-lived.
Forgive us, renew, and empower us to stand
and to strive and to struggle for Christ
    and the kingdom. **Amen.**

YOU KNOW

Father, you know who and what we are and what we are not.
You know our confusion and our falling.
You know our strengths and our shame.
You know our professions of hope and
    just how quickly we lose heart.
You know our failure to stand firm on the faith we proclaim
and our criticism of others who fail.
You know our complaints when we suffer
and our refusal to share one another's hurts.
You know our self-satisfaction, our self-
    interest, and our selfishness
and the conflict between our good intentions
    and our love of the easy way forward.
You know the battles we failed to win
because we were never quite sure just whose side we were on.
Forgive us that we lose the struggle so easily
because we insist on standing in our own
    strength and not in our Lord's.
Forgive us, restore us, and reclaim us as
    your own, through Christ. **Amen.**

OUR DARKNESS

Father, so often our darkness is of our own making.
Much of the pain and loss we face is
    because of our own foolishness.
We act all surprised when we are filled with despair.
We are alone and afraid, but have wandered far from you.
Forgive our wandering off on our own,
forgive our foolish attempts at self-reliance.
Here and now we confess that without you
there is no health, no hope, and no way home.
Forgive us for walking in dark places
    and bringing darkness

to those that we love.
Forgive us, cleanse, renew, and reclaim us.
We thank you for your welcome which we never deserve
and for the cross of Christ,
before which we now stand. **Amen.**

SELF-CONFIDENCE

Father, forgive our self-confidence,
    our foolish self-reliance,
and our empty self-satisfaction which is
    lost in the first wave of defeat.
Forgive us the poverty of our faith and the
    weakness of our hold on you
which is too easily broken by pain and despair.
Forgive us our too easy victories and our desire
to win friends and influence people that is crushed
by the first word of critical comment.
Forgive us and keep us from self-pity
    when things go wrong
and give us your mercy, your hope, and a
    share in Christ's victory of love.
Give us the strength to support one another,
the power to grow in faith,
and the love and determination to offer
    hope to our neighbours.
In the name of Christ the Lord, who sets us free. **Amen.**

FORGIVE

Father, forgive us every failure to love
    our neighbours as ourselves;
forgive every thoughtless word,
every selfish thought, and every unkind deed;
forgive all our refusals to be open to your Spirit
and to allow him to make our lives new;

forgive us our failure to enter into the victory of Christ
by our refusal to carry the cross.
Father, open our eyes, our ears, our hearts, and our minds
and by your grace make us into the
    people you meant us to be
from the very beginning.
We ask this not only for our own benefit
    but for your glory. **Amen.**

LIKE PALM SUNDAY

Father, we confess that we,
    like the crowds on Palm Sunday,
have praised Jesus so easily one day
and just as easily, like Peter, have denied him the next.
We confess that we have chosen to follow him one day
but allowed the direction of our
    commitment to be changed
by the pressure of the crowd.
We confess that though we find it easy to
    praise him when we are together
we find that our thoughtless, selfish words and
    deeds still nail Christ to his cross.
We confess that we find the ways of the
    world too easy and undemanding,
but following Christ involves a path to a cross.
Forgive us our easy excuses as we continue to be
his Pilate and Herod and his Judas and Peter;
condemning, ignoring, betraying, and
    denying the one who is Lord.
Forgive our weak faith and commitment
and make us the true followers we long to be. **Amen.**

PRAYERS FOR ALL AGES

KING OF CREATION

Lord, we praise you because you are
    the King of all creation.
There is no one and nothing greater than you.
You are greater than anyone who has ever lived,
greater than anyone who is yet to be born,
and you are greater than anyone who
    is living in the world today.
We thank you because you use your greatness
to make a world worth living in.
You planned your world to be a good place
where we can find happiness, joy, and real life.
It was your intention that everyone should feel
loved, wanted, and of real value.
You meant everyone to live in freedom and without fear.
You made your world and filled it
with hills and valleys, seas and oceans, streams and rivers,
plants and animals, birds and insects, fish and fruit.
All went well until you made us
and allowed us the freedom to make our own choices.
We have chosen to please ourselves
and we have broken the laws you gave for our good
and we have spoilt your world as we have spoilt our lives.

Lord, we thank you that you loved
    us enough to send Jesus
so that through his life, death, and resurrection
we might enter the kingdom of your love.
Lord, we do not find it easy to follow Jesus
and we are often tempted to give up or give in.
We pray that you will fill us with your Holy Spirit
that we may have the courage and strength
to be faithful to Jesus and to trust him
    when the going gets tough.
We ask this in Jesus' name. **Amen.**

KNOWING YOU

Heavenly Father, we praise you for your
    power and for your truth
and that it was always your plan
that we should live knowing you and your love for us,
that you always meant us to know that
you are on our side and that you are not against us.
We praise you for your power which created the world
and for your love which is always reaching
    out to make our lives complete;
that you are the one
from whom everything that is good, true,
    and worthwhile has its beginning.
Wherever we find joy, hope, and love,
we know that in the beginning it came from you alone.
Wherever we find people who do good things
    and are helpful, loving, and kind,
it is because you are working in their hearts and lives
even if they do not know you.
We thank you for the stories of Jesus in the Bible
and how they show us that even he faced
    all kinds of pain and problems

and also rejection because he was faithful to you.
We thank you that he died in our place to break down
the barriers between us that our selfishness had built.
We praise you for his resurrection and for the promise
that nothing will ever be able to defeat your love for us.
We praise you that even when we feel surrounded
by people who do not know you and
    do not want to know you,
we can still be sure that you are with us
and that you will never leave us
as you give us the courage, strength, and love we need
to stand firm with him.
We ask this in his name. **Amen.**

WE PRAISE YOU

Heavenly Father, we praise you
because you are so great and so very wonderful.
We praise you for all that you are
and we thank you for all that you do.
We praise you for making the whole world
and we thank you for holding everything in your hands.
We praise you that you are perfect and pure and holy
and we thank you that you love us so much.
We praise you that you know us completely
and we thank you for loving us still.
We praise you for coming in Jesus
and we thank you that he came to make our lives new.
We praise you that he knows what it
    is like to live in this world
and we thank you that he knows the things
    that hurt us and make us afraid.
We praise you for his life, death, and resurrection
and we thank you that he lived, died,
    and suffered for us all.

We praise you for those who help us when we are hurting
and we thank you for those who hold us when we are sad.
We praise you for those who stand by us
when everything seems to be going wrong
and we thank you for those who never stop caring
even when we make a mess of our lives.
We praise you for those whose words and deeds
make others aware of your love
and we thank you for those whose care and understanding
help others to have hope and peace and love.
We praise you that nothing will ever stop you loving us
and we thank you that Jesus has told us
to show and to offer his love to others.
We ask by your Holy Spirit
that everything we say and do will
  praise your name. **Amen.**

SOMETIMES

Heavenly Father, we praise you because you
  have always been there for us.
Sometimes we are not aware of your presence
and we live as if you did not exist,
yet you still break into our lives
and make yourself known even when we least expect it.
We praise you for coming to us when we
  are afraid and for giving us hope
and for being with us when no one else can be there
and when no one else wants to be.
We praise you for life's wonderful surprises
that bring us great excitement and a tremendous thrill.
We thank you for the pleasure that new
  things can bring to our lives
and for the encouragement they bring;
for the joy of making new friends,

starting a new school, or learning something new.
We praise you for the new things that
>   Jesus taught us about you
and your wonderful love for us all,
and for that time on the mountaintop
when his disciples discovered something new about him.
We praise you for those times in our lives
>   when we find we can trust you
and for those times when we know for
>   certain you are with us,
and for how Jesus' disciples shared their knowledge
that he was far, far greater and far, far more wonderful
than they had ever thought possible.
Forgive us that our faith is so small and weak
and that we do not use it every day.
Fill us with your Holy Spirit so that
>   everything we say and do this week
may open someone's eyes to see Jesus in us. **Amen.**

PASSION SUNDAY

You are our amazing God!
We praise you for the way you make us see life
and the things in our lives in a whole new way,
and for the way you help us to see that the things
that were once so important to us
do not really matter so much after all.
We praise you for the way you open our eyes
to see the wonder of your world
and our ears to listen to the song that
>   creation sings to your glory.
We thank you most of all for your Son, Jesus Christ,
through whom you go on changing our hearts, our minds,
and the way we think about things.
On this Passion Sunday we remember

his life of goodness, healing, teaching, and love
and we remember his death on the
> cross for us, in our place.

We praise you that though in the eyes of his enemies
he was defeated, he was the victor,
and that though those who hated and rejected him
thought that they had won, he was the
> one who was victorious.

We praise you that he showed us that your love for us
will never be defeated and your concern for our lives
will never come to an end.

We praise you that whenever we look at the cross
we can know what he did for us
and we thank you for all those who down the years
have remained faithful to God no matter
> what others said or did.

Forgive us that we find it so easy to give up and to give in.
Come, fill us with the strength of Jesus
and keep us faithful to him that our lives
> may be filled with his victory.

In Jesus' name. **Amen.**

PRAYERS OF INTERCESSION

ASH WEDNESDAY

We pray for those who are ashamed of themselves
and of what they have done;
for those whose words and deeds have
   made others ashamed of them;
for those whose mistakes are known to everyone
and for those whose failures are known only to you;
for those who are filled with despair and a sense of defeat
because of the mess they have made of their own lives
or because of the behaviour of those that they love.
May the presence of Christ give them peace.
Lord, in your mercy,
hear our prayer.

We pray for those who are depressed and despairing;
for those who once were filled with
   hope and great expectations
and for those whose plans and dreams
   have come to nothing;
for those who feel crushed and broken and empty
and for those with no one to help or understand;
for those tormented by doubts and fears and temptations
and for those whose thoughts and moods
   and feelings are filled with darkness.

May the presence of Christ give them joy.
Lord, in your mercy,
hear our prayer.

We pray for those who are filled with regret
and for those feeling lost and alone;
for those whose sadness seems unending
and for those whose brokenness seems beyond repair;
for those whose words hurt themselves and others
and for those whose deeds are designed to spoil
what could have been good;
for those whose selfishness and self-centredness
are a source of pain to others
and for those who have no idea
of the anguish, worry, distress, and pain
they are causing those who have loved them most.
May the presence of Christ bring them to their senses.
Lord, in your mercy,
hear our prayer.

We pray for those who are trying to come to terms
with a serious illness
and for those who are finding it simply too hard to bear;
for those whose illness is terminal
and who can find no peace and no hope;
for those who, knowing they are dying,
are ready to meet with God;
for those who are sharing the suffering of others,
who care for the sick and the elderly
    and give dignity and love,
and for those who are frail in body or in mind.
May the presence of Christ give them hope.
Lord, in your mercy,
hear our prayer.

We pray for ourselves
and for all that is troubling our hearts and our minds,
for all that takes away our peace;
for our need of God's guidance and strength
in the face of the growing demands made upon us
and the stress that we face every day;
for the Holy Spirit to open our eyes,
    our ears, and our minds
to the great things he is longing to do
    in and through our lives;
for every new beginning we are offered
and for every chance to offer worship
    and witness and service
in the name of him who makes all things new.
May the presence of Christ fill us with power.
Lord, in your mercy,
hear our prayer.

Through Christ our Lord. **Amen.**

FACING CONFLICT

I ask your prayers for all who face conflict;
for those for whom life is an endless struggle;
for those who are uncertain where their
    next meal will come from,
or if it will come at all;
for those for whom life seems dark and empty
and for all who are hungry in our greedy, selfish world;
for those sent away from the rich
    nation's table empty-handed
although there is enough for all.
The Lord hears our prayer.
Thanks be to God.

I ask your prayers for all who face conflict;
for those who are persecuted
and all who are tortured and imprisoned
    for their faith in Christ.
I ask your prayers for all who are neglected, ignored,
or made to feel as if they do not count.
I ask your prayers for those who, for the sake of others,
stand against injustice, corruption, and evil
and do so at great cost to themselves.
The Lord hears our prayer.
Thanks be to God.

I ask your prayers for all who face conflict;
for homes where life is one long argument,
where the members of families cannot agree together;
for relationships that began in love and hope
but have been soured by broken promises
    and where trust has been lost;
for those facing violence, hatred, or indifference;
for those who long ago were robbed of their innocence
and for those hurting still.
The Lord hears our prayer.
Thanks be to God.

I ask your prayers for all who face conflict;
for those who have a conflict within;
for those who find it hard to love or be loved
because they have never been loved from the first;
for those whose lives are in turmoil
yet the smile on their face hides the hurt
    and the pain deep inside;
for those filled with loss and with sadness
and for those for whom the bottom has
    dropped out of their world;

for those filled with anger and with bitterness;
for those crushed with doubts and fears;
for those with no sense of their own value
and no joy in the friendship of others
because they are locked up in themselves.
The Lord hears our prayer.
Thanks be to God.

I ask your prayers for all who face conflict;
for those whose sickness has broken their spirits
and for those whose ill-health has worn them down;
for those whose illness has restricted
    the lives of their families
and for those who have lost their freedom
as they are concerned for the old and infirm;
for those who take up the battle
to bring wholeness, healing, renewal, and hope;
for those who are committed to prayer and to love.
The Lord hears our prayer.
Thanks be to God.

We bring our prayers in the name of Christ,
who shares all our conflicts. **Amen.**

THINK OF SOMEONE

Think of someone who is suffering;
someone whose whole life has been damaged
by the words and deeds of someone else;
someone who is filled with resentment
because of what they have suffered;
someone who suffers still, through no fault of their own.
May the hope of God be with them now.

Think of someone who is suffering;
someone whose whole life has been changed by war;

someone who has been taught to hate others
not the same as themselves;
someone whose attitudes and values
are crippling life for themselves and those around them.
May Christ be their peace.

Think of someone who is suffering;
someone who was always fit and well;
someone facing a terminal illness;
someone caring for those that they love;
someone with a past that now haunts them,
an uncertain future, and a today they can't face.
May the mercy of God enter into their fear.

Think of someone who is suffering;
someone whose suffering is unseen and unknown to others;
someone who has been so deeply hurt
they simply cannot share it;
someone whose tears are deep inside;
someone who has been let down and left alone;
someone filled with a grief that is too much to bear.
May the pierced hands of Christ hold them now.

Think of someone who is suffering;
someone imprisoned for their faith
or for standing up for what they know is the truth;
someone locked in by their disability and a society
that is blind to their needs;
someone locked out by their lack of education
or their colour of skin;
someone locked up in the poverty trap.
May Christ be the key to their being set free.

Think of someone who is suffering.
Think of yourself;

think of the hurt that is in your own heart and mind;
think of the affection you long to receive;
think of your hopes that came to nothing;
think of your pain that no one knows;
think of the prayers that seem unanswered;
think of the joy, love, thanks, and peace
that have always sustained you;
think of the person you always wanted to be.
May the love of Christ be in you now.

Lord, in your mercy,
hear our prayer.

In the name of Christ, who suffered for us all. **Amen.**

WE PRAY

Father, we pray for the world where
    men and women are lost
and children are unloved and afraid
and for the world where people worship
anyone and anything rather than their Maker;
for the world in its need of hope and renewal
and for the world where might is right
and the weak are crushed.
We pray for the world wherever there is darkness.
We pray for the world in need of the
    transforming light and life of Christ.
The Lord hears our prayer.
Thanks be to God.

We pray for our community where many feel forgotten.
We pray for those around us who are empty
and hurting and broken and lost;
for those around us who feel on the scrapheap of life
and for those whose skills are no longer needed

and who have time on their hands.
We pray for our community where many are isolated
by their lack of ability, their poverty,
   or their failure to be loved
and for our community where many long
for acceptance, love, understanding, and hope.
The Lord hears our prayer.
Thanks be to God.

We pray for the church.
We pray for the one church of Jesus Christ.
We pray that we may be one in him.
We pray that our witness, our worship,
and our service may be worthy of him.
We ask for wisdom, understanding, truth, and sensitivity
in the whole of our life together in Jesus.
We pray for the joy and the wonder of knowing
that our fellowship here is designed for eternity.
We pray that this church will be a home for sinners
and a place where all are made welcome
and where people are made whole in Christ.
The Lord hears our prayer.
Thanks be to God.

We pray for any we know to be in need;
for those who are ill, those who will never recover,
and those who wait with them;
for those facing important decisions
and for those unsure of what tomorrow will bring.
We pray for our neighbours, our families and friends,
and any we know who need to hear of the love of God,
to feel the touch of the grace of the Lord
   Jesus Christ upon their hearts,

and to experience the life-changing
> power of the Holy Spirit.

The Lord hears our prayer.
Thanks be to God.

We pray for ourselves.
We pray for all we must do and say and face
in the coming days of this week.
We pray for the words of faith we should share
and the prayers for others we need the words for.
We pray for the challenges that we know we must face
and the pressures and pain and stress of each day.
We ask for the transforming love of Christ to go with us.
The Lord hears our prayer.
Thanks be to God.

In the name of Christ, who makes all things new. **Amen.**

A WORLD IN NEED

Almighty God, our heavenly Father,
we pray for those who walk in the way of Jesus;
for those who refuse to compromise with evil
and for those who stand firm in his name;
for those who are committed to your
> kingdom of love and peace

and those who are prepared to pay the price
of naming the name of Jesus with their lips and their lives.
We pray for the victory of joy.
This is our prayer.
We ask it in Jesus' name.

We pray for all those whose hearts and
> minds are filled with violence;

for those whose actions bring pain
> and confusion to many;
for those involved in guerrilla warfare and for terrorists
who see only the cause for which they are fighting
and not the price others are paying
in their heartache and in the destruction
> of all that matters to them.
We pray for the victory of peace.
This is our prayer.
We ask it in Jesus' name.

We pray for all who are ill;
for the lonely, the lost, and the despairing.
We pray for all who mourn and for all whose
> ambitions have come to nothing.
We pray for all who experience loss of work, loss of home,
loss of freedom, loss of courage, and loss of love.
We pray for those whose lives now feel empty and
for whom joy is a thing of the past.
We pray for the victory of hope.
This is our prayer.
We ask it in Jesus' name.

We pray for those who find themselves
> standing where Jesus stood;
for those overwhelmed by crucifying
> hatred and indifference
and for those who are rejected because of
> their commitment to Christ.
We pray for those who are gentle in a
> world where might is right
and for those who are determined to
> go on caring and loving
even when it costs all they have.

May they remember Christ's promise that
> the meek will inherit the earth.

This is our prayer.
We ask it in Jesus' name.

We pray for those like Pilate who think more of themselves
and their own desires and neglect
> responsibilities they once accepted.

We pray for those who, like the soldiers,
hide behind rules and orders
and for those like the Chief Priests
who turn a blind eye to their own double standards.
We pray for those like Jesus' disciples
who, when things get tough, just run away.
We pray for those, like the thief on the cross,
whose trust in Christ opens the door into heaven.
This is our prayer.
We ask it in Jesus' name.

We pray for ourselves.
As Christ triumphed over sin and death for us
and turned the world's understanding
> of victory upside down,

so we pray, Lord, touch our lives with your love
and transform them by the power of the Holy Spirit.
Use even our lives, our words, and our deeds, we pray,
as a message of hope to our neighbours.
May your light shine in us and through us
and bring honour and glory to your name.
This is our prayer.
We ask it in Jesus' name.

We ask all our prayers in the name of
> him who died for all. **Amen.**

YOU HAVE A PURPOSE

Father, you have a purpose for all your creation.
Jesus said, 'It is finished,' and we believe that in him
you have accomplished it.
In him you have shown us that the way to life
is through humble, crucified love.
We pray for those who find this way hard
  and have fallen by the wayside.
May the love of Jesus warm hearts that once
  loved you but now have grown cold.
Lord, in your mercy,
hear our prayer.

We pray for those whose lives are cold and empty
because they are too ambitious for themselves;
for those who see life and success simply
in terms of the things of earth and in material possessions;
for those who long to see your goodness, truth, and love
flow into every corner of life
and for those who are finding the path
  Christ calls them to follow
too painful to bear.
May the gentle, insistent voice of Christ call them still.
Lord, in your mercy,
hear our prayer.

We pray for all those who are committed
to the love and care of their neighbours;
for those whose choices and decisions
  affect the lives of many people;
for all politicians and leaders who are
  genuinely seeking the good
of those they were appointed to serve;
for those who care for others in the community,

those who are paid and those who do it voluntarily;
for those who have become indifferent
    to the needs of others
and for those who are filled with
    arrogance and impatience.
May the compassion of Christ transform all their service.
Lord, in your mercy,
hear our prayer.

We pray for all who are committed to Christ;
for those who follow him in spite of opposition
and who name his name in the face of ridicule;
for those who are counting the cost of
    loving Christ and their neighbours
and those who are turning their backs upon both;
for those who are ready to sacrifice
    their own personal freedom
to enrich the lives of those without hope;
for those who are discovering the reality of your love
in the face of prejudice, fear, and greed.
May they be filled with the joy of their Lord.
Lord, in your mercy,
hear our prayer.

We pray for those whose vision of love,
    service, and obedience
has been drowned out by the sound of achievement
and clouded over by selfish ambition.
We pray for those weighed down by the threat
or reality of persecution for their faith;
for those crushed by fear or neglect;
for those whose Palm Sundays end
and who enter their Gethsemane
and find they have been given a cross;

for those who lack the strength, courage,
> and faith that they need
to complete the journey.
May the presence of Christ keep them
> safe to the end, and beyond.
Lord, in your mercy,
hear our prayer.

We pray for any we know who are
> facing times of great testing;
for those whose faith and hope are
> being pushed to the limit
and for those whose faith and love
are too weak and vulnerable to take
> much more of the strain.
We pray for the church all across the world
and our fellow Christians in our local community.
We pray for this church and all its faithful people.
We pray for ourselves that our songs and our service
and our glad hosannas may ring in endless
> praise to him who alone is worthy.
Lord, in your mercy,
hear our prayer.

In the name of the Prince of Peace. **Amen.**

PRAYERS OF COMMITMENT

WE COMMIT OURSELVES

Father, we are all too well aware that the world
is full of wilderness experiences.
We commit ourselves to love those in need of affection,
to hold those who are hurting,
to listen to those who are lonely,
to speak the truth to those who are mistaken,
to stand with those who are standing alone,
and to walk with those who have lost their way home.
Give us your compassion, your wisdom, your strength,
and your victory that we may be Christ
> to our neighbours. **Amen.**

A NEW FOCUS

Lord, we commit ourselves
to keep our eyes focused on Christ,
our ears open to your word,
our lives open to your Spirit,
and our hearts open to your love. **Amen.**

WE OFFER

Lord, we offer you our suffering
so that we can receive your patience and courage.

We give you our pain so that you can transform it.
We offer you our brokenness so that you can heal it.
We give you our emptiness, Lord, come and fill us. **Amen.**

OUR HEARTS AND MINDS AND LIVES

We offer our hearts and minds and lives to
   the Christ who transforms us.
We pray for the power of the Spirit to
   go on working through us
and to give us the joy of seeing all other
   lives made new. **Amen.**

MOMENTS

Father, every day has its moments of testing and difficulty;
every situation is filled with opportunities
   for service and witness.
We commit ourselves to carry the cross that you give us.
Enable us to give you all the glory and praise. **Amen.**

TO FOLLOW

Lord, we commit ourselves to follow Christ
not only on days that feel like Palm Sunday
but when he calls us to follow him to Calvary.
We commit ourselves to follow him always
   and only and for ever. **Amen.**

PRAYERS OF DISMISSAL

GO INTO THE WORLD

Go into the world and stand with those who are tempted;
go into the world and hold those who are falling;
go into the world and love those who are breaking;
go into the world in the power of the Spirit;
go into the world in the name of Christ
 who defeated the tempter. **Amen.**

SEND US OUT

Fill us with joy, send us out in hope;
fill us with power, send us out with your word;
fill us with your presence,
 send us out for our Lord. **Amen.**

THE NEEDS OF OTHERS

Go into the world with
your eyes open to the needs of others,
your ears ready to hear their cry,
your lips ready to speak the name of Jesus,
and your heart longing to share his love. **Amen.**

IN THE NAME OF CHRIST

Go now in the name of Christ

and the power of the Spirit,
for the Lord is with you—always. **Amen.**

FROM THIS PLACE

We go from this place in the name of Jesus.
In all our trials and problems he will be with us.
Whatever we face and wherever he leads us
we can be certain he knows the way
    and he will love us. **Amen.**

GO NOW

Go now in the knowledge of his love,
    his truth, and his glory.
Go now in the strength of his word.
Go now in the power of the Spirit
    to name him as Lord. **Amen.**

ABOUT THE AUTHOR

David Clowes, born in Ellesmere Port, left school at fifteen following a secondary modern education. In 1965 he committed his life to Christ at Heaton Mersey Methodist and in 1967 he received God's call into the Methodist ministry. He trained at Hartley Victoria College and gained a degree in theology at the University of Manchester.

David served in a number of churches in the northwest of England before retiring in 2010 after thirty-five years in active ministry. His first book, *500 Prayers for All Occasions*, began as a spiritual exercise during a sabbatical. This was followed by *500 More Prayers for All Occasions*. His third book of prayers, *500 Prayers for the Christian Year*, is based on scriptures from the Revised Common Lectionary.

David is married to Angela, and they have two married sons, a foster son, and four grandchildren.